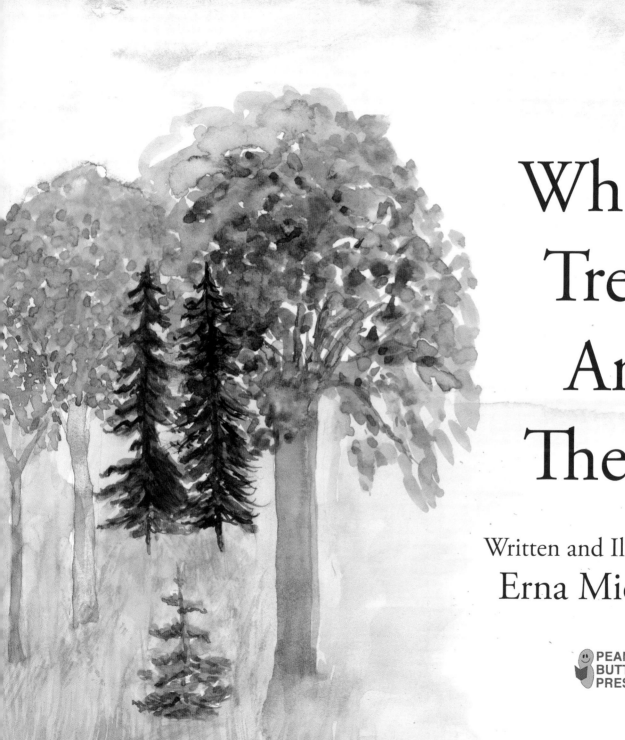

# Whose
# Trees
# Are
# These?

Written and Illustrated by
## Erna Michalow

 PEANUT
BUTTER
PRESS

Peanut Butter Press
9-1060 Dakota Street
Winnipeg, MB R2N 1P2
www.peanutbutterpress.ca

Book design by Rosemary Ellis

Printed and bound in Canada by Friesens Corporation ❧
The binding of this hardcover edition is sewn.

Library and Archives Canada Cataloguing in Publication

Michalow, Erna
Whose trees are these? / written and illustrated by Erna Michalow.

ISBN 978-0-9865329-7-9

1. Trees--Juvenile literature.  I. Title.

QK475.8.M53 2012          j582.16          C2012-907334-2

Dedicated to Daniel, Eric and Thomas
who also love trees.

Whose Trees Are These?

"Mine," said the Sun.
"I am the powerful light
which gives the leaves their colour.
The trees need my heat.

"They must have my light.
They turn my light into life.
Oh mine, all mine, all mine,"
beamed the Sun.

7

Whose Trees Are These?

"Mine," said the Rock.
"The tree roots stretch into my crevices.
With time I break down into sweet, rich soil for plants.
I talk to the trees of old bones,
of my many layers,
of deep, hidden things.
Mine, mine, mine," rumbled the Rock.

9

Whose Trees Are These?

"Mine," said the Earth.
"I feed the trees to help them grow.
I hold them steady and firm.
I allow oxygen to reach their roots so the trees have energy.
I help the trees send messages into the roots of other tree families.
Mine, mine, mine," murmured the Earth.

11

# Whose Trees Are These?

"Mine," said the Water.
"I wiggle my way up inside the trees.
I push food into their leaves to the very tips.

13

"I splash rain to bathe the leaves in summer.
In winter I turn into blankets of snow to cover the trees.
Mine, mine, mine," burbled the Water.

Whose Trees Are These?

"Mine," said the Air.
"I touch them everywhere.
I give the trees the carbon dioxide
and oxygen they need.

"I clean the leaves and spread seeds
when I become the wind.
I send whispering voices of love.
Mine, mine, mine,"
breathed the Air.

19

Whose Trees Are These?

"Mine," said the Fire.
"I blaze trees into campfires.
I burn the trees for heat.
I pop the pine cones for fun.
I scorch the trees so forests will regrow.
**Mine, mine, mine,**" crackled the Fire.

21

Whose Trees Are These?

"Ours," said the Animals.
"They are our homes—
our nests, burrows and webs.
They are our playground
for swinging and leaping.
They are safe.

"They are food for us—fruits and nuts,
roots and bark, leaves and sap.
Ours, ours, ours,"
laughed the Animals.

Whose Trees Are These?

"Ours," said the People.
"We need trees to build our homes
and furniture—beds, tables and chairs.
We press them into paper and tap into them for maple syrup.
They shade our streets and parks.
They clean the air we breathe.

"We marvel at their beauty.
We feel peaceful.
**Ours, ours, ours,**" insisted the People.
"Oh yes! Ours."

But the trees replied,
"We belong to no one
and to everyone.
We are touched by all—

The Sun
The Rock
The Earth
The Water
The Air
The Fire
The Animals
The People.

"We reach up.
 We stretch down.
 We spread our arms outward.
 We hold our strength inward.
 We move across each other.

"We hug. And we dance.
We are connected,
in this world, to
ALL
THAT
IS."